The Little Seahorse

Written by Sheri Fink

Illustrations by Mary Erikson Washam

Books by Sheri Fink:

The Little Rose
The Little Gnome
The Little Firefly
Exploring the Garden with the Little Rose
The Little Seahorse

*This book is dedicated to my
beautiful mother, Judy, and all the
mothers living within our hearts.*

To the memory of my mother—M.E. Washam

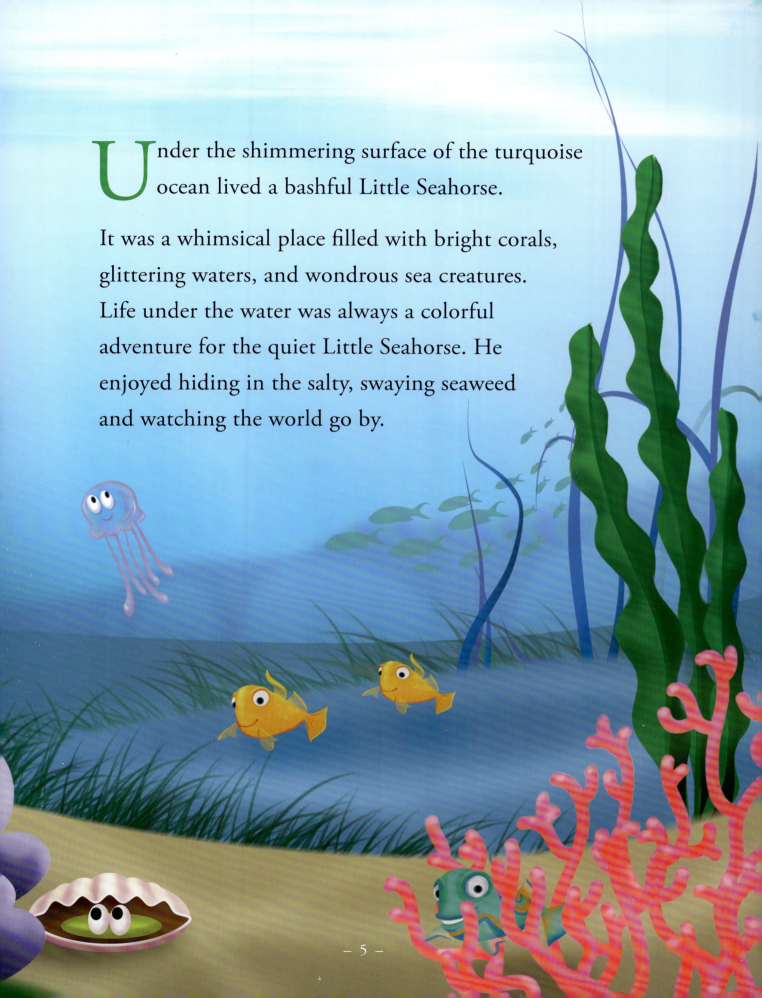

Under the shimmering surface of the turquoise ocean lived a bashful Little Seahorse.

It was a whimsical place filled with bright corals, glittering waters, and wondrous sea creatures. Life under the water was always a colorful adventure for the quiet Little Seahorse. He enjoyed hiding in the salty, swaying seaweed and watching the world go by.

One day, while happily exploring the ocean floor
and watching the sunbeams dance through the waves,
the Little Seahorse drifted upon something mysterious
glimmering radiantly in the sunlight. It was a brilliant
white orb nestled in the brown sugar sand.
He was intrigued.

The Little Seahorse poked it with his nose and tail.
It was very hard! He tried to play with it, but quickly
realized it was much too heavy to be a ball. He was
captivated by its beauty, and wondered what he could
do with this strange and beautiful object.

The Little Seahorse imagined giving this precious orb
to his mother. He had never given her a present before.
He loved his mother very much and wanted to show her
how much he appreciated her. He nearly leapt out of
the water with excitement at this idea!

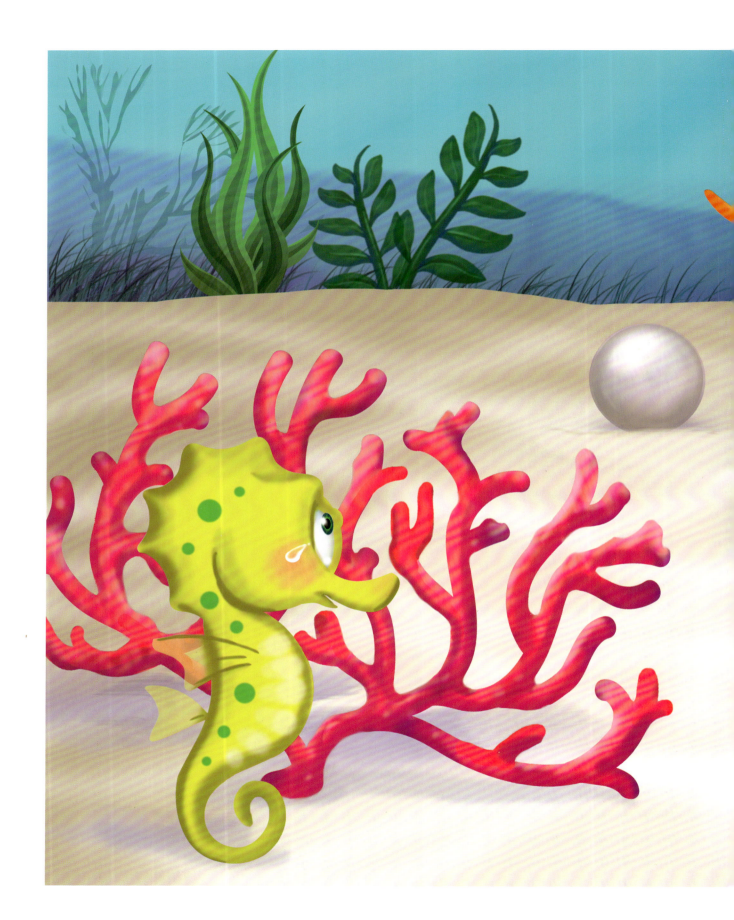

Suddenly, he heard unfamiliar voices. Who was coming? The Little Seahorse felt scared and darted behind a bright pink coral while keeping an eye on his magnificent discovery.

Two large pipe fish were swimming by and stopped to admire the Little Seahorse's treasure. He watched the pipe fish try to pick up the orb.

What if they took it? His chest was tight, as though he couldn't breathe. He felt a bubble rise in his throat as tears started to roll down his hot, red cheeks.

He wanted to stop them, but he wasn't sure what to do. He just knew that he really wanted to give this special object to his mother.

He pictured his mother's loving smile and remembered how she always encouraged him to be brave. He courageously dashed out into the open water, right in front of the bigger fish. They seemed surprised to see the Little Seahorse. He didn't know what to say. He was scared to speak up for himself, but he was even more afraid of losing his wonderful prize.

He felt embarrassed to be crying and started to stutter as he desperately reached for the words. He took a slow, deep breath and explained to the pipe fish that he had found the shiny orb before them, and that it was a present for his mother.

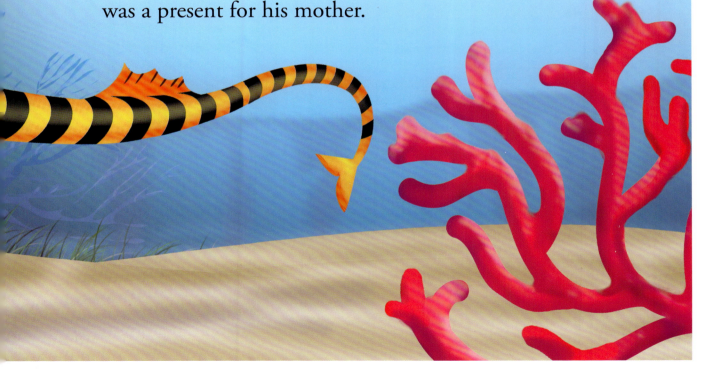

The pipe fish listened to what the Little Seahorse had to say. He cried as he bravely told the fish about how wonderful his mother was, and how much she deserved this special gift.

Touched by the Little Seahorse's story, the pipe fish agreed it would make a fantastic present. They said they were inspired to do something special for their mothers as well.

As they were saying good-bye and swimming away, the Little Seahorse felt relieved and happy that he had been brave. Even though they were bigger and stronger, the pipe fish were really nice. The Little Seahorse was glad to make new friends.

Then, he felt panicked when he realized
he had no way to move the orb
on his own.

Although he was afraid to ask, The Little Seahorse was determined to bring it home for his mother. He anxiously called out to the friendly pipe fish to see if they would assist him. He could feel his little heart pounding nervously as he awaited their response. Thankfully, the fish swam back and agreed to help.

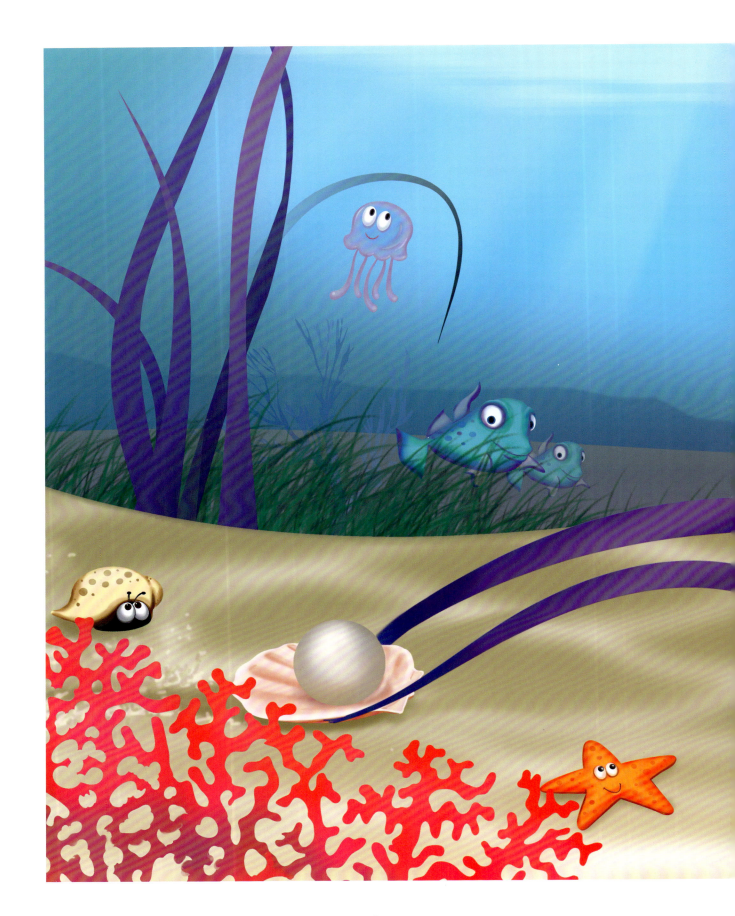

It took some time to figure out how to carry it, but with creativity, teamwork, shells, and seaweed, the three of them were able to carefully transport the precious object through the cool waters toward the Little Seahorse's home.

Along their journey, other sea creatures noticed this unusual procession and were curious about it. The object was unique, and looked important. More and more fish followed the trio. Some of them even pitched in to help! Everyone wanted to see where they were taking it.

At first the Little Seahorse felt nervous about all of this attention. In the past, he didn't like to stand out in the crowd. And here he was at the front of this unexpected underwater parade!

When they finally stopped at his home, the group
gathered around to see what would happen next.
The Little Seahorse was uncomfortable with everyone
watching him, but he was also excited to present this
one-of-a-kind gift to his mother. So he mustered up the
courage, and called for his mother to come outside.

She was surprised by the colorful crowd assembled outside her front door. The Little Seahorse bravely presented the extraordinary orb to her in front of everyone. She knew right away that it was a rare and beautiful pearl. All of the sea creatures cheered!

The Little Seahorse's mother was delighted with his thoughtful gift, and was even happier that her son had overcome his shyness in order to give it to her. She was always very proud of him -- especially today.

He thanked his new friends for their help. Seeing his mother enjoying her new gift made him feel glad that he was courageous.

He looked around admiring the blissful scene: the smiling faces of his new friends, the vibrant colors and beauty of his ocean neighborhood, and the joy in his mother's eyes. The Little Seahorse was grateful to be a part of such a wonderful underwater world, and lived happily ever after.

Just like the Little Seahorse, you can choose to be courageous. Always speak up for what you want, even if you feel nervous asking for help. When you are brave and ask for assistance, you have the opportunity to make new friends. The world becomes a happier and friendlier place for everyone.